JEFF
BEZOS

Founder of Amazon.com

by Jamie Weil

Content Consultant
Anthony Rotolo, Professor
S. I. Newhouse School of Public Communications
Syracuse University

Core Library

An Imprint of Abdo Publishing
www.abdopublishing.com

www.abdopublishing.com

Published by Abdo Publishing, a division of ABDO, PO Box 398166, Minneapolis, Minnesota
55439. Copyright © 2015 by Abdo Consulting Group, Inc. International copyrights reserved in
all countries. No part of this book may be reproduced in any form without written permission
from the publisher. Core Library™ is a trademark and logo of Abdo Publishing.

Printed in the United States of America, North Mankato, Minnesota
082014
012015

Cover Photo: Mark Lennihan/AP Images
Interior Photos: Mark Lennihan/AP Images, 1, 34, 37, 45; Reed Saxon/AP Images, 4; Amazon/
AP Images, 7; Ross D. Franklin/AP Images, 8; H. Armstrong Roberts/ClassicStock/Corbis, 10;
Fotoreport Quelle AG/dpa/Corbis, 14; Evan Agostini/AP Images, 17; TinaImages/Shutterstock
Images, 19; AP Images, 21; Barry Sweet/AP Images, 26; David McNew/AP Images, 30 (top
left), 30 (top right), 30 (bottom left), 30 (bottom right); Kristoffer Tripplaar/Sipa USA/AP
Images, 32; Red Line Editorial, 38; Ted S. Warren/AP Images, 40

Editor: Arnold Ringstad
Series Designer: Becky Daum

Library of Congress Control Number: 2014944235

Cataloging-in-Publication Data
Weil, Jamie.
 Jeff Bezos: founder of Amazon.com / Jamie Weil.
    p. cm. -- (Newsmakers)
 Includes bibliographical references and index.
 ISBN 978-1-62403-640-8
 1. Bezos, Jeffrey--Juvenile literature. 2. Amazon.com (Firm)--Juvenile literature. 3. Internet
bookstores--United States--History--Juvenile literature. 4. Electronic commerce--United
States--Biography--Juvenile literature. 5. Businessmen--United States--Biography--Juvenile
literature. 6. Electronic books--History--Juvenile literature. 7. Kindle (Electronic book reader)-
-Juvenile literature.
 1.Title.
 381.4500092--dc23
 [B]
                                                                    2014944235

CONTENTS

CHAPTER ONE

WHO IS JEFF BEZOS?

Jeff Bezos is full of surprises. When he was interviewed on the television news show *60 Minutes* in December 2013, he proved it. He told the news team he had a secret. He claimed they would never guess what it was. He told them if they could guess it, they must be very lucky. With that kind of luck, he said, he would give them half his money and send them to a casino. Bezos, the

Bezos, the founder of Amazon.com, believed his latest project would revolutionize the way people shop online.

founder of the shopping website Amazon.com, has an estimated net worth of more than $25 billion. He was confident they couldn't guess his secret.

Bezos was right. The news team had no idea what the secret could be. At the end of the interview, Bezos took them into a room in Amazon Lab126. This research and development department in Cupertino, California, is where his company studies new ideas. Inside the news team saw Bezos's visionary plan for the future of package delivery. There were several small flying robots, known as drones. Each had eight helicopter-like rotors, spinning blades that propel it into the air. The robots were black and yellow with long, spidery legs.

On the Cutting Edge

Inside Lab126, a screen appeared in front of the group. A video revealed why Amazon was building these drones. It showed how Amazon would deliver packages in 30 minutes or fewer. This is far faster than the delivery trucks used today. The drones would use

Amazon's drones are capable of carrying five-pound (2.3 kg) packages up to ten miles (16 km).

the Global Positioning System (GPS) to find their way from warehouses to customers' homes. This is the same navigation system many cars use today. Bezos was careful to note that the drones were not yet ready to begin deliveries. Many tests needed to be done first. It could be years before a drone delivered a real package. Still, Bezos felt confident this was the next big advancement in online shopping.

Bezos has been the biggest name in online shopping for more than a decade. Amazon.com was his first entry into this industry. The website made

Amazon sells millions of unique products, shipping them from its many enormous warehouses.

him a billionaire. Its success helped drive the growth of online shopping. Amazon is an online store where people can buy things and have them delivered. From books to food, the website sells nearly every kind of product. If Bezos's drone project works, these products will reach buyers faster than ever before.

Early Life

Jeff was born on January 12, 1964, in Albuquerque, New Mexico. His mother, Jacquelyn Gise, was married for only a short time to his biological father, Ted Jorgensen. Bezos has no memory of him.

Instead Bezos thinks of Miguel Bezos as his father. Miguel, also known as Mike, married Jacquelyn in 1968 when Jeff was four years old. Mike legally adopted Jeff at that time. Two years later, his sister, Christina, and brother, Mark, were born.

Jeff's parents recognized his creativity when he was three years old. One day Jacquelyn found him playing with a screwdriver. He was trying to turn his crib into a bed.

The Infinity Cube

Jeff loved to build things, especially toys. At age 12, he became interested in a toy called the Infinity Cube. In this clear box, rotating mirrors create the illusion of an endless tunnel. However, the $22 cost was too much for the family budget. Jeff figured out which parts he needed to buy and built his own toy for less.

When Jeff was a child, computers were much larger and more difficult to use than they are today.

When Jeff was four, the Bezos family moved to Houston, Texas. Jeff spent summers with his mother's parents on a ranch in Cotulla, Texas. Jeff's grandfather, Lawrence Preston Gise, nurtured Jeff's ingenuity. Together they fixed bulldozers, cared for cattle, and repaired windmills. Jeff's skills grew as he spent his summer days on the ranch.

A Talented Student

Jeff liked school, and he excelled at it. His teachers noticed he was very bright. He was placed in the advanced student program at Houston's River Oaks Elementary. In 1974, when Jeff was in fourth grade, his school got a computer. Computers were new to most people, and the teachers didn't know how to use them. Jeff stayed after school and figured out how to make the school's computer work. This experience sparked Jeff's interest in computers.

He also loved building things. Jeff became skilled at rigging traps throughout the house. To keep his siblings from entering his room, he made a buzzer that would sound whenever they opened his door.

By high school, Jeff had moved to Miami, Florida, with his family. He graduated from high school in 1982 at the top of his class and gave a speech on graduation day. During his speech, Jeff talked about becoming a space entrepreneur. He envisioned space hotels and space stores. He felt it would be good for people to have options in case something happened to the planet Earth and they needed to leave.

After high school, Jeff enrolled at Princeton University. There he planned to study physics. However, advanced physics classes were hard for him.

Princeton University

Princeton University is a private research university located in Princeton, New Jersey. It is one of the oldest and most prestigious colleges in the United States. The physics program, which drew Jeff to Princeton, is famous. Seventeen Princeton physicists have won the Nobel Prize, one of the highest honors in science.

FURTHER EVIDENCE

Chapter One includes information about Amazon's plans to use drones for package delivery. Why might Bezos want to build these drones? What evidence from the chapter supports this point? Take a look at the website below. It features more information, photos, and videos about Amazon's plans. Does the material on the site support the evidence from the chapter? Does it make you think of more challenges Bezos and Amazon might face with their drone plans?

Amazon Prime Air
www.mycorelibrary.com/jeff-bezos

He changed his plan. Jeff graduated from Princeton in 1986 with a degree in electrical engineering and computer science.

CHAPTER TWO

GOING WEST

After Bezos graduated, he worked in New York City in the finance field. He eventually noticed a trend that would change his life. The Internet, a global network of computers that made it possible to communicate cheaply and quickly, had been invented in the 1960s. By the early 1990s, the Internet was growing at an incredible rate. Bezos hit upon the idea of opening an online store.

Bezos believed an online store had the potential to change the way millions of people shopped.

Taking a Risk

The only problem was that Bezos already had a high-paying job. He was also scheduled to receive a hefty bonus at the end of the year. In 1993 he had married MacKenzie Tuttle, who worked with him in New York City. He needed to consider her feelings. MacKenzie said she would support him no matter what. Bezos had to make this hard choice by himself. He used a method he often used for hard decisions. Bezos called it a Regret Minimization Framework. He imagined himself at 80 years old. Then he asked that version of himself which decision would leave him with the fewest regrets.

Bezos decided if he didn't take the risk, he would regret it. Now he needed to decide what to sell on the Internet. He made a list of 20 options. Bezos considered things such as software, books, and clothes. After analyzing his choices, he picked books. Selecting books would allow Bezos to sell a wide selection of one type of product and build customer

Bezos and MacKenzie have been married since 1993.

trust. It would be impossible to sell every product right away, but books would give him a good start. With millions of books in print worldwide, he had plenty of products to sell.

On Independence Day weekend in 1994, Bezos and MacKenzie flew to Texas. There they picked up a car given to them by Bezos's father. MacKenzie drove them to Seattle, Washington. Bezos sat beside her and wrote a business plan on his laptop. Two factors made Seattle an attractive choice for Bezos's new company. First, many talented computer programmers lived there. Second, the

In the 1990s, Seattle became a major hub for growing Internet companies.

company would be close to a major book distribution warehouse.

What's in a Name?

On the way to Seattle, Bezos contacted an attorney to help him set up his company. The attorney asked Bezos what he wanted the company to be called. Bezos suggested "Cadabra," as in the magicians' phrase "Abracadabra." The attorney thought Bezos had said "cadaver," meaning a dead body. Bezos didn't want customers to mishear his company's name in the same way. But he needed to register his company name soon. On July 5, 1994, he registered it under the temporary name "Cadabra."

In the following weeks, Bezos considered new names. He wanted the name to start with an *A* so it would come up first in online directories. These websites helped users find information on the Internet before search engines such as Google became popular. The directories often listed sites alphabetically. Bezos studied the *A* section of the dictionary for ideas. Finally he settled on "Amazon," after the largest river in the world.

Setting Up Shop

Now that he had a name, Bezos needed money for his venture. He held 60 meetings with potential investors. He told them there was a 70 percent chance his plan would fail. The first question most people asked was,

http://home.netscape.com/

RE COURIER

Netscape announces the first open, cross-platform "digital envelope" protocol, to be supported by Intuit, MasterCard, an others.

WS 95 NAVIGATOR BETA

Download the latest beta release of Netscape Navigator, specially tuned to take advantage of Win 95 interface enhanceme and features.

RMANIA

Test drive a fully loaded Netscape Commerce or Communications Server for 60 days and win the race for business serve solutions. Now **free** for educational and charitable nonprofit institutions.

WELCOME TO NETSCAPE!

EXPLORING THE NET
What's New
What's Cool
Net Directory
Net Search

NETSCAPE STORE
Software
Support
Publications

COMMUNITY
Netscape User Groups
Internet White Pages

In 1995 Web browsers and the Internet were much simpler than they are today.

"What's the Internet?" Still, Bezos was a persuasive speaker. He ended up with about 20 people who invested $50,000 each. In the end, saying yes made these original investors very wealthy. Bezos's parents contributed a large portion of the money. They gave approximately $300,000 they had saved for retirement.

On the way to Seattle, Bezos had stopped in Northern California to interview his first potential employee. This was Shel Kaphan, a brilliant computer programmer. He had already been involved in several Internet companies. Kaphan agreed to join Bezos's company in Seattle.

Bezos and MacKenzie turned their two-bedroom Seattle apartment into Amazon headquarters. The garage became a work space with three computers. Bezos decided to save money on desks. Rather than buying new ones, he built his own using wooden doors. Amazon became famous for its door desks. Bezos says they are a symbol of spending money only on what matters.

Growing Pains

Amazon.com officially launched its website on July 16, 1995. A team of 300 of Bezos's friends and family had tested it beforehand. Bezos told them to spread the word. There was no other advertising. Bezos felt Amazon was going to be huge someday. But he did not realize how fast it would grow. In the first 30 days, Amazon sold books in all 50 states.

The Amazon team was not prepared. Most

Amazon's Culture

In Amazon's corporate offices in Seattle, the buildings are unmarked. They blend in with other businesses on the street. Inside Amazon's logo hangs on the wall behind a long rectangular desk. On one side of the desk sits a bowl of dog treats for employees who bring their dogs to work. This tradition started when early employees worked very long days. One couple, Eric and Susan Benson, didn't want to leave their dog, Rufus, at home. Bezos promised Rufus would always be welcome.

of the ten paid employees had other day jobs. They packed boxes late into the night. Bezos took action quickly when employees made suggestions. One night Bezos told a fellow packer that kneeling down to fill boxes was killing his knees. He said they needed kneepads. The employee responded that they needed packing tables. Bezos thought that was a brilliant idea. The next day, the company had new packing tables.

During these late nights, orders were filled until the delivery company's last pickup of the day. Obsessed with customer service, Bezos wanted to fulfill every order as fast as he could. He drove the packages to the shipping location himself.

This chapter talks about taking big risks to follow a dream. When Bezos decided to start Amazon, he used his own Regret Minimization Framework. He described the process in an interview:

> So, it really was a decision that I had to make for myself, and the framework I found which made the decision incredibly easy was what I called—which only a nerd would call—a "regret minimization framework." So, I wanted to project myself forward to age 80 and say, "Okay, now I'm looking back on my life. I want to have minimized the number of regrets I have." I knew that when I was 80 I was not going to regret having tried this. . . . I knew that if I failed I wouldn't regret that, but I knew the one thing I might regret is not ever having tried.
>
> Source: "Jeff Bezos Interview." Academy of Achievement. Academy of Achievement, May 4, 2001. Web. Accessed July 2, 2014.

Consider Your Audience

Read the passage and think about what Regret Minimization Framework means. Bezos uses this method for many of his hard choices. How would you explain this method to another audience, such as your friends?

CHAPTER THREE

AMAZON EXPLODES

A mazon's success changed the way books were sold. Bezos had pioneered a new path. Many established booksellers followed him. Two months after Amazon.com launched, it was selling $20,000 worth of books each week.

In its first year, the company spent more money than it made. This left Amazon with a $303,000 loss. Bezos needed more money to stay in business.

In its first few years of operation, Amazon sold only books.

He approached investors called venture capitalists and asked for money. Venture capitalists invest money in small businesses they think may grow. In December 1995, venture capitalists invested $981,000 in Amazon.

From the beginning, Bezos was much more concerned about growth than profit. Even when the company earned money, Bezos reinvested it back into the business. His theory was that waiting longer for a return would give him an edge because other businesses are rarely so patient.

In November 1997, Amazon opened its first fulfillment center in New Castle, Delaware. This was a massive warehouse where goods could be stored for shipping. In 1998 Amazon began selling movies and music. In 1999 it began selling electronics, toys, and games. The selection of products continued to expand into the early 2000s. All of these products had to be stored somewhere. Amazon built dozens of fulfillment centers all over the world.

The fulfillment centers are organized in seemingly random ways. For example, a toy car may be stacked next to a dictionary. They may both sit across from a laptop computer. Mixing items like this maximizes the use of space.

Branching Out

As Amazon grew, Bezos began to expand into new areas. One new project, called Blue Origin, involved building spacecraft. At first the project was top secret. In 2005 a reporter discovered a research facility south of Seattle. After this Bezos announced his plans. He walked into a local newspaper office and gave an interview to the unsuspecting editor. Blue Origin's goal is to make it affordable and safe for humans to

Person of the Year

In 1999, just five years after Bezos started Amazon, he was named *Time* magazine's Person of the Year. The recognition goes to the person who made the biggest impact on the news that year. At age 35, Bezos was the fourth-youngest person to be named Person of the Year. *Time* made the decision because of how Bezos changed the way people shop.

Amazon fulfillment centers usually look like normal warehouses on the outside.

Conveyer belts are used to move items through the huge facility.

Employees use tricycles to get from place to place quickly in Amazon's largest fulfillment centers.

Shipping, sorting, and shelving processes all use computers to ensure accuracy and speed.

Looking inside Amazon

These photos show the exterior and interior of an Amazon fulfillment center. Computers tell workers where to sort things so that every inch of space is used. The fulfillment centers have grown larger and larger as Amazon has expanded. What did you expect a fulfillment center to look like after reading about it in Chapter Three? How do these photos differ from your expectations?

visit space. The company shows that Bezos never forgot the vision he talked about in his high school graduation speech.

Another Amazon venture grew out of the company's unique needs. Millions of products were being stored, tracked, and sold. Bezos had his workers develop a sophisticated computer system to handle all this data.

Amazon later realized it could make money renting its computing power to other companies. The company launched Amazon Web Services (AWS) on March 14, 2006. This is a group of different computer-related services. For example, a company

Amazon Web Services

Amazon Web Services sells computer services to other companies. Many Internet companies use Amazon's systems. A few include Netflix and Pinterest. The US government uses the services as well. AWS is by far the largest provider of this kind of service. In 2013 the company announced it was 5 times larger than its 14 largest competitors combined.

Amazon Web Services has offices all over the world.

might purchase storage space or computer processing power. Amazon sells these services over the Internet. AWS brought in approximately $2.2 billion in revenue for Amazon in 2012.

Jeff Bezos was called "tech's most enduring innovator" by *Time* magazine. In the issue, colleague Peter Thiel wrote about Bezos:

> *Twenty years ago, Jeff Bezos left a lucrative job in finance to drive across the country and start his own business. He went on a wild ride: from original hero of Internet commerce to poster child of dotcom hype. . . . Amazon is still the greatest tech story of the 1990s; it's also one of a few contemporaries still run by its founder. Nobody else reinvests almost every cent of profit in growth, as Bezos still does. Amazon is immensely valuable today, and almost all of its value comes from the future. The journey ahead for Jeff Bezos is just as great now as when he first set out in 1994.*
>
> Source: Peter Thiel. "Jeff Bezos." Time. Time, April 23, 2014. Web. Accessed July 2, 2014.

Point of View

The writer views Bezos in a very favorable way. What does he say makes Bezos such a standout innovator? Read back through this chapter. Do you agree? Why or why not?

more as another river skimmer passed. The people dancing on its deck didn't spot the rope stretched from bridge to shore. They never did. New pretties were always having too much fun to notice little things out of place.

When the skimmer's lights had faded, Tally tested the rope with her whole weight. One time it had pulled loose from the tree, and both she and Peris had swung downward, then up and out over the middle of the river before falling off, tumbling into the cold water. She smiled at the memory, realizing she would rather be on that expedition—

CHAPTER III.

A Caucus-Race and a Long Tale

They were indeed a queer-looking party that assembled on the bank—the birds with draggled feathers, the animals with their fur clinging close to them, and all dripping wet, cross, and uncomfortable.

The first question of course was, how to get dry again: they had a consultation about this, and after a few minutes it seemed quite natural to Alice to find herself talking familiarly with them, as if she had known them all her life. Indeed, she had quite a long argument with the Lory, who at last turned sulky, and would only say, 'I am older than you, and must know better'; and this Alice would not allow without knowing how old it was, and, as the Lory positively refused to tell its age, there was no more to

kindle

Shay's voice came back sleepily. "So soon, Tally-wa? I'm having *fun.*"

"I think I got a Smokey."

"You sure?"

"Positive. She smells like laundry."

"I see her now," Fausto's voice cut through the music. "Brown shirt? Dancing with that guy?"

"Yeah. And she's *tanned.*"

There was an annoyed, distracted sigh, a few mumbled apologies as Shay disentangled herself from her ugly boy. "Any more?"

Tally scanned the crowd again, making her way around the girl in a wide circle, trying to catch another whiff of smoke. "Not as far as I can tell."

< Books

kobo

FULL OF SURPRISES

As Amazon grew, Bezos thought of new ways the business could sell products. Amazon sold products that were delivered by trucks. But what if it could deliver products over the Internet? In the early 2000s, Bezos hit upon the idea of using an electronic reader, or e-reader. These devices allow users to read books on screens. They can hold thousands of books. At the time, e-readers were not

Bezos believed e-readers could drive sales of e-books through Amazon.

popular. But Bezos believed they would revolutionize the way people read. He launched the development of Amazon's own e-reader device.

He wanted his e-reader to be easy enough for anyone to use. He also wanted it to be inexpensive. His plan was to sell the device at a low cost. Bezos planned to earn money on the project by selling e-books through Amazon.

Bezos put a team together and sent them to Lab126. The device they made became known as the Kindle.

The Kindle

After much trial and error, Amazon launched its first Kindle e-reader

Electronic Ink

The Kindle's screen uses technology known as electronic ink. Most computer and tablet screens use electricity whenever they are on. This can drain batteries quickly. Electronic ink screens are different. Electricity moves tiny particles inside the screen. Depending on where a particle is, that part of the screen appears dark or light. Electricity is only used when the particles move. This means that the screen only uses power when the page changes.

The original Kindle cost $399 when it was released, but later versions started at less than $100.

in November 2007. Kindle gave people a new way to buy and read books. Today there are many Kindle devices with different features and prices. The user has the ability to download e-books directly onto the device.

Between the Kindle and the online bookstore, Amazon disrupted the traditional bookselling industry. Physical stores couldn't compete with Amazon's prices and selection. Many small, independent booksellers closed. The industry landscape was changing, whether

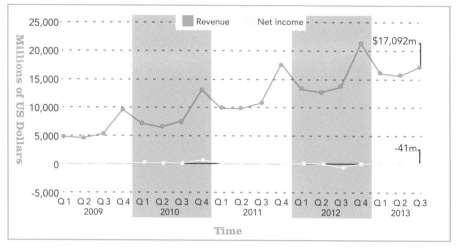

Revenue, Growth, and Profit

This graph shows Amazon's revenue, the amount of money it takes in. It also shows the company's net income, which is Amazon's total revenue minus its expenses. These figures are shown from 2009 to 2013. How does the graph demonstrate Bezos's views about growth and profit? Why do you think revenue peaks around the same time each year?

people liked it or not. Amazon didn't apologize. It prided itself on disrupting the traditional ways of doing things.

Surprising the World

Bezos took the world by surprise when he purchased a newspaper, the *Washington Post*, in August 2013. He spent $250 million. With the newspaper industry struggling, it seemed like a strange choice. In an interview, Bezos said the owner of the newspaper convinced him he was the right person to own it. For years Bezos had been using Amazon to publish books on the Kindle. Now he owned his own major publication.

In June 2014, Bezos announced Amazon's latest device. The Fire Phone was a new smartphone designed with deep connections to Amazon's store. One notable feature of the phone is called Firefly. Users can point the phone's camera at objects to identify them. The system recognizes millions of objects. If the item can be purchased on Amazon's website, the user can do so right from the phone.

Best Business Person of the Year

Fortune magazine named Bezos its 2012 Business Person of the Year. The magazine selected him because he takes risks and disrupts industries. His patient business philosophy has made Amazon a massive company. It has also made Bezos a very wealthy man.

Bezos introduced the Fire Phone at a special event on June 18, 2014.

Bezos Today

In 2014 Bezos turned 50. He still lived in Seattle with MacKenzie and his four children. His innovative spirit first emerged when he tried to rebuild his crib as a child. It has evolved into building drones to deliver packages. His patience has made him successful.

His heroes are animator Walt Disney and inventor Thomas Edison. Bezos likes Edison for his brilliant inventions and Disney for his ability to inspire others. Bezos has been able to combine both those traits to change the way the world shops.

EXPLORE ONLINE

Chapter Four talks about Jeff Bezos's purchase of the *Washington Post*. The article at the website below goes into more depth on this topic. Does the article answer any of the questions you had about Bezos's decision?

Jeff Bezos and the *Washington Post*
www.mycorelibrary.com/jeff-bezos

IMPORTANT DATES

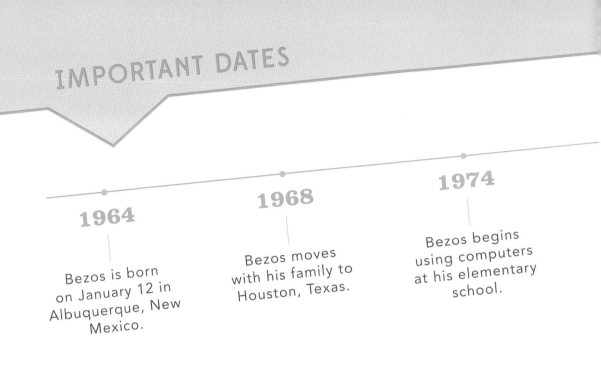

1964
Bezos is born on January 12 in Albuquerque, New Mexico.

1968
Bezos moves with his family to Houston, Texas.

1974
Bezos begins using computers at his elementary school.

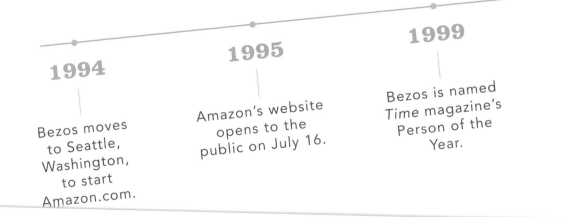

1994
Bezos moves to Seattle, Washington, to start Amazon.com.

1995
Amazon's website opens to the public on July 16.

1999
Bezos is named *Time* magazine's Person of the Year.

1982

Bezos graduates from high school in Miami, Florida.

1986

Bezos graduates from Princeton University.

1993

Bezos marries MacKenzie Tuttle.

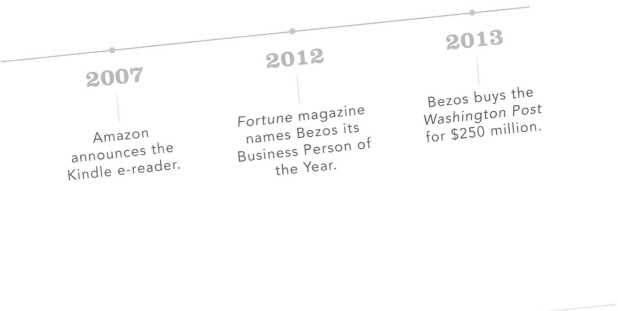

2007

Amazon announces the Kindle e-reader.

2012

Fortune magazine names Bezos its Business Person of the Year.

2013

Bezos buys the Washington Post for $250 million.

Take a Stand

Bezos thinks of his childhood as ideal. He looks back fondly on summers working the ranch with his grandfather. He worked the land, fixed things, created inventions, and read. Today kids are having more and more of their experiences online. Do you think kids would benefit from a childhood like the one Bezos had? Or do you think doing things online can be just as good? Why?

Tell the Tale

Several times in his life, Bezos had an innovative idea and ran with it. Following a dream often takes risk and creativity, along with careful planning. Imagine you are starting your own business. Write 200 words explaining your business to a potential investor. What does your business do? What would you name it? What kind of risks would be involved?

Surprise Me

Chapter Four discusses Bezos's projects both inside and outside of Amazon. Which project surprised you the most? Write a few sentences about why it surprised you.

You Are There

This book discusses how Jeff Bezos made an effort to cut down on expenses when starting Amazon.com. Imagine you are an early employee of the company seeing the door desks for the first time. What would you think about Bezos's attitude? Would it make you want to continue working there? Write a paragraph describing how you feel.

GLOSSARY

cadaver
a dead body

minimization
the act of making something
as small as possible

entrepreneur
a person who starts a
business

physicist
a scientist who studies matter
and energy and the way they
interact with each other

envision
to imagine something you
believe may happen in the
future

venture
a new project that typically
involves risk

visionary
seeing clear ideas about what
should happen or be done in
the future and acting upon
those

ingenuity
a strong skill for inventing
things

LEARN MORE

Books

McClafferty, Carla. *Profiles: Tech Titans*. New York: Scholastic, 2012.

Ryan Jr., Bernard. *Jeff Bezos*. New York: Ferguson, 2005.

Websites

To learn more about Newsmakers, visit **booklinks.abdopublishing.com**. These links are routinely monitored and updated to provide the most current information available.

Visit **www.mycorelibrary.com** for free additional tools for teachers and students.

INDEX

ABOUT THE AUTHOR

Jamie Weil lives in a small rural town in Northern California. Like Jeff Bezos, she spent time on a cattle ranch in her youth.